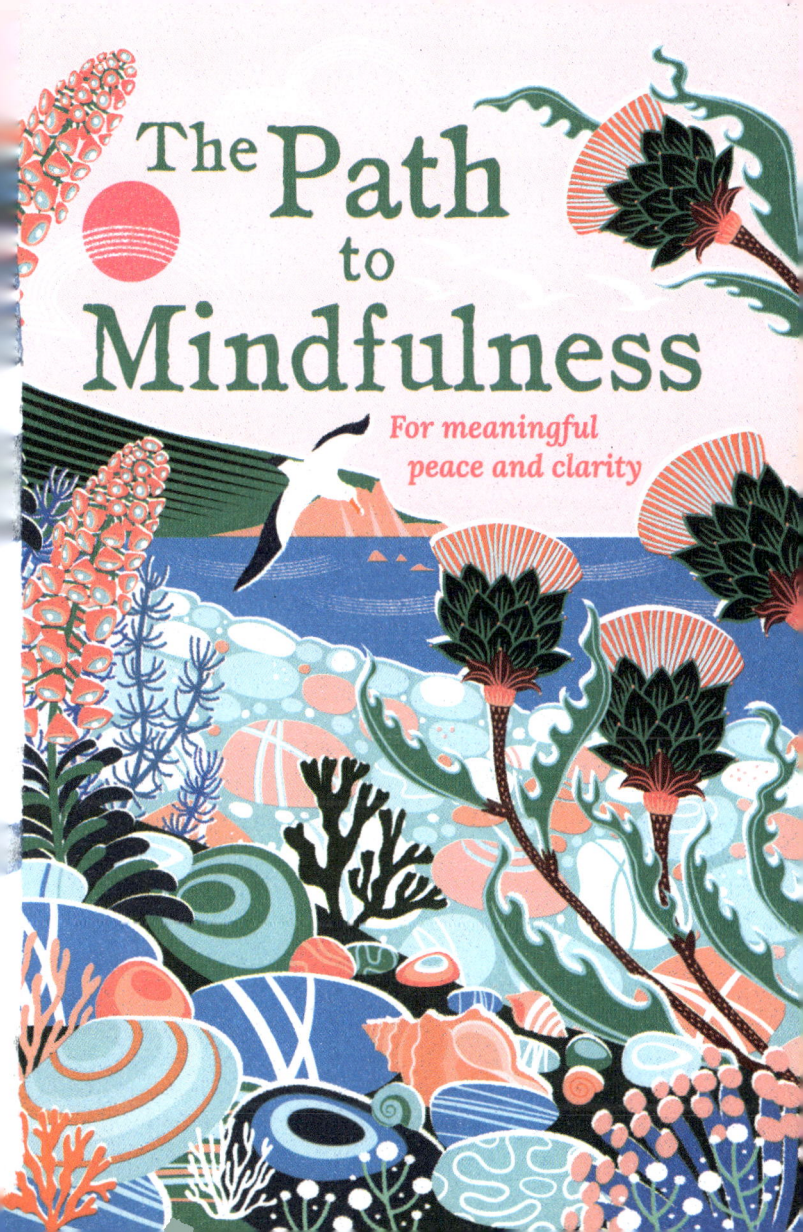

for all your gift books and gift stationery

This edition first published in Great Britain in 2024
by Allsorted Ltd., WD19 4BG.

All rights reserved. No part of this work may be reproduced in any form or by any means, electronic or mechanical, including photocopying, recording or by any information storage and retrieval system, without the prior written permission of the publisher.

All information in this publication is for educational and informational purposes. It is not intended as a substitute for professional advice. Should you decide to act upon any information in this publication, you do so at your own risk. While the information in this publication has been verified to the best of our abilities, we cannot guarantee that there are no mistakes or errors.

© Susanna Geoghegan Gift Publishing

Author: Rebecca Dickinson

Illustrator: Jo Parry
Cover and concept design: Jo Parry and Nick Pettit
Contents design: Blackbird Brands

ISBN: 978-1-915902-55-9

Printed in China

10 9 8 7 6 5 4 3 2 1

Hello

The modern world can be a stressful place. Noise, news, notifications, traffic, people, crowds, sirens, responsibilities, emails, deadlines, information, work, places to be, things to do, stuff to sort out, more notifications; there is just soooo much going on. It. Never. Stops.

All these demands and distractions can make it hard for us to switch off, causing us to feel anxious and overwhelmed. But prolonged exposure to stress isn't just bad for our health and wellbeing, it can prevent us from enjoying all the incredible things life has to offer.

Fortunately, there is an antidote to our frantically busy lives that doesn't involve narcotics, alcohol or escaping to a tropical island. The answer is mindfulness.

Mindfulness is simply a state of awareness. By embracing a more present, focused, mindset, and by using mindfulness techniques in your daily life, you will discover how to replace stress and anxiety with peace, clarity and balance. This book will help you to do just that.

"Tell me, what is it you
plan to do with your
one wild and precious life?"

Mary Oliver

"Wherever you are,

be there totally."

Aristotle

What is mindfulness?

It's easy to rush through life on auto-pilot, without stopping to notice what's really around us. The practice of mindfulness is the opposite of this.

Mindfulness involves paying attention to the present moment, without judgement. By calmly acknowledging our thoughts, feelings and bodily sensations, we can engage with the world around us more fully and experience things we might have been taking for granted. It could be as simple as feeling the sensation of water on your skin as you take a shower, or noticing the shapes of the clouds.

By training your mind to focus, you will also be able to step away from the chatter inside your head. This will help you to enjoy living in the here and now, instead of dwelling on the past or worrying about the future.

Mindfulness is a technique that is rooted in science. Studies show that it calms the amygdala – the part of the brain that's activated by fear and stress. So, by nurturing a mindful mindset, you can learn to replace feelings of unease and anxiety with calmness and clarity.

"Mindfulness means being awake. It means knowing what you are doing."

Jon Kabat-Zinn

"HOW WE PAY ATTENTION TO THE PRESENT MOMENT LARGELY DETERMINES THE CHARACTER OF OUR EXPERIENCE AND, THEREFORE, THE QUALITY OF OUR LIVES."

Sam Harris

Nurturing your mindset

In recent years, the term 'mindful' has become part of our common vocabulary. You've probably seen mindfulness memes and quotations on social media. You might even have tried some mindfulness techniques yourself. When you are feeling anxious or overwhelmed, exercises – like guided meditations and breathing techniques – can be a great way to help you calm down and manage your feelings in any particular moment.

However, mindfulness isn't just a trend; neither is it something that should be reserved for wellness classes and retreats. That's because true mindfulness isn't just something you do, but something you are. The key is to develop a mindful mindset, which will set the tone for your whole life.

We can't always make stressful events go away, but we can change the way we perceive them. Turning mindfulness into a habit will give you the capacity to deal with whatever life throws your way, helping you to feel at peace with yourself and the world around you.

> Mindfulness is an effective self-help measure for coping with, and resolving, stress. But if your emotional issues are ongoing or are severely impacting your life, ask your doctor or a therapist for professional support.

"You don't have to control your thoughts. You just have to stop letting them control you."

Dan Millman

"Within you, there is a stillness and a sanctuary to which you can retreat at any time and be yourself."

Hermann Hesse

The benefits of mindfulness

Mindfulness has its roots in Buddhism, but you don't need to be spiritual or religious to embrace it; you just need to be willing to practise.

A huge amount of research shows that mindfulness is a powerful way to improve your physical and mental health, enriching every area of your life. Incorporating mindfulness into your daily life can help you to:

- sleep better
- understand your emotions and manage negative thoughts
- improve concentration and brain function
- reduce the symptoms of depression and anxiety
- cope with pain
- manage negative thoughts

- fight infection by boosting your immune system
- enjoy better relationships
- increase your happiness and enjoyment of life.

Mindfulness helps you to maintain a state of positive mental wellbeing. Throughout this book we will explore different techniques that you can use in both daily life and times of difficulty to help soothe anxiety, reduce stress, boost feelings of contentment and improve mental clarity and awareness.

> For most people, mindfulness can be extremely beneficial; however, occasionally, it can make symptoms worse, for example, if you've experienced trauma. Speak to a doctor or a trained therapist before starting if you are unsure.

"The mind is everything.
What you think, you become."

Buddha

"The curious paradox is that when I accept myself just as I am, then I can change."

Carl Rogers

Understanding anxiety

Anxiety is something we all experience from time to time: it's a natural response to stress or to a perceived threat. When we're faced with a stressful situation, our bodies automatically switch into 'fight or flight' mode, causing adrenalin to be released into the bloodstream. Although adrenalin can be useful – for example, if we need to stay alert or react quickly to a dangerous situation – it's often produced when we don't need it, which leads to the physical symptoms that can accompany anxiety. These symptoms can include:

- headaches
- feeling dizzy, faint or panicky
- sweating
- shortness of breath
- tingling, trembling or shaking

- a racing heartbeat or palpitations
- feeling tearful
- feeling cold
- feeling weak
- stomach ache or an upset tummy.

The good news is that research shows mindfulness can be a powerful tool for easing anxiety. What's more, by incorporating mindfulness into your everyday life, you can learn to lessen the impact of stressful events in the first place.

> **Feeling anxious can be a perfectly normal reaction, but if anxiety is getting in the way of your daily life or affecting your health, it's important to get professional help.**

"Your calm mind is the ultimate weapon against your challenges. So relax."

Bryant McGill

"Everything is created twice,
first in the mind and then
in reality."

Robin Sharma

Getting started

There are many mindfulness techniques, including guided meditations, yoga and breathing exercises. All these practices help you to become more aware of your thoughts, feelings, bodily sensations and breath, enhancing your mental wellbeing.

You don't have to subscribe to a formal class or course to reap the benefits of mindfulness; you can also learn to develop mindfulness in your daily life by following these steps at home.

- Begin by finding a quiet, comfortable place to sit.

- Notice your thoughts. Watch how they come and go like clouds in the sky.

- Simply observe your thoughts, without engaging with them or judging them.

- Let your thoughts drift through your mind, noticing how they flow in and out of their own accord.

- Imagine creating a space between you and your thoughts.

- Finally, imagine letting these thoughts go. Watch them float away.

In time, you may discover that distancing yourself from your thoughts in this way can help you to feel calm and relaxed.

Did you know?
Studies suggest that our minds naturally wander around 50% of the time.

"Where wisdom reigns,
there is no conflict between
thinking and feeling."

C.G. Jung

Focus on breathing

Life starts with our first breath and ends with our last. Yet, although breathing keeps us alive, unless you have a health condition that affects your breathing, most of the time we just take it for granted.

However, focusing on the breath is one of the foundations of mindfulness. That's because the way you breathe is closely connected to your state of mind. You've probably noticed that when you're stressed or anxious, your breathing becomes faster and shallower. This sets off alarm bells in the brain, activating the 'fight or flight' response, which, in turn, triggers a rise in stress hormones, blood pressure and heart rate. It's a two-way system: feeling stressed causes you to breath more rapidly and breathing more rapidly triggers a physiological reaction that makes you feel even more stressed.

However, by learning to consciously control our breathing, we can switch off the 'fight or flight' response and engage the parasympathetic nervous system instead. This is the part of the nervous system that releases calming hormones into our veins, helping us to feel happy and relaxed.

"Breathe. Let go. And remind yourself that this very moment is the only one you know you have for sure."

Oprah Winfrey

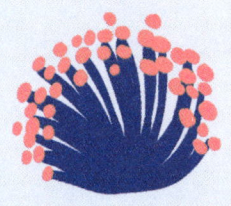

"Breathe in deeply to bring your mind home to your body."

Thích Nhất Hạnh

Get to know your breath

This very gentle exercise is a simple way to nurture a sense of awareness of your breath.

- Start by becoming aware of the sensation of your breath. Don't try to change or control it; simply notice your natural breathing pattern.

- Pay attention to the air as it enters your nostrils. Notice how it's cool on the inhale and warm on the exhale. Observe the rise and fall of your belly and chest.

- Notice whether your breath flows smoothly or erratically. Don't try to alter it or force it; just observe how it travels freely through your body.

- If your mind wanders – which it probably will – simply bring your attention back to your next breath. Keep doing this every time you get distracted, without judging yourself.

You can pay attention to the pattern of your breathing almost anywhere – when you're on the bus, walking the dog, hanging out the washing, doing the school run, or waiting for a doctor's appointment. Bring your awareness to your breath whenever you need to realign yourself with the present moment.

"Breath is the bridge which connects life to consciousness, which unites your body to your thoughts."

Thích Nhất Hạnh

"As long as we are fortunate enough to be breathing, we will breathe through, breathe deep and breathe out."

Taylor Swift

Get in touch with your vagus nerve

Imagine if there was such a thing as a relaxation button; a control switch that was at your disposal 24 hours a day, free of charge, no batteries required. Just one click could calm your nerves and soothe your mind. Well, meet your vagus nerve! This wonderful bundle of neurons is like a direct line to inner peace – and mindfulness is one of the most effective ways to activate your vagus nerve and stimulate vagal tone. It's worth taking a moment to find out more about this amazing piece of human engineering.

- The vagus nerve is the longest nerve in the body. In Latin, vagus means 'to wander', and this cranial nerve wanders from your head, down your neck, through your chest and into many of your organs.

- It's part of your parasympathetic nervous system, which activates your relaxation response, instructing the body to 'rest and digest'.

- Stimulating the vagus nerve is a biological way to counteract the body's 'fight or flight' stress response.

- Activating the vagus nerve triggers a surge of calming brain chemicals. This helps your breathing to slow down, causing a drop in your heart rate, blood pressure and stress levels.

"The first and greatest victory is to conquer self."

Plato

"If it's out of your hands,

it deserves freedom

from your mind too."

Ivan Nuru

Become a belly breather

A great way to stimulate the vagus nerve is by taking some deep, abdominal breaths – also known as 'belly breathing'. Breathing in this way interrupts the 'fight or flight' response and activates your relaxation response, decreasing your heart rate, blood pressure and reducing levels of the stress hormone cortisol.

- Find a quiet spot and lie on your back or sit in a comfortable position.

- Place one hand on your chest and the other on your belly. Your shoulders and hands should be relaxed.

- Take a deep breath in through your nose, then out through your mouth. Does your belly gently rise and fall? If so, you're breathing into your abdomen. Continue breathing in this way.

- If your chest hand rises, focus on breathing into your abdomen on your next inhale, so that the hand on your belly rises and the one on your chest stays almost still.

- Repeat for up to 10 minutes, until you are able to do it confidently. If your attention wanders, just bring it back to your breath.

Try to practise belly breathing regularly until it becomes a habit.

"Let go of the battle.
Breathe quietly and let it be.
Let your body relax and
your heart soften."

Jack Kornfield

Check in with your body

Your body and mind are intimately connected, like two sides of the same coin. However, there are times when we need a little reminder of this.

Doing a body scan reconnects the mind and body, drawing us into the present moment. Take a few minutes now to check in with yourself. You can do this lying down or sitting quietly in a chair, with your eyes closed.

- Bring your attention to your breath, noticing the rise and fall of your belly.

- When you're ready, turn your attention to your feet, taking in any sensations, such as the way they make contact with the floor, whether they feel warm or cool. Just observe, without judging.

- Move your attention slowly up your body – to your ankles, calves, knees, thighs, and so on – examining each part of your anatomy.

- Keep scanning, observing any sensations, any discomfort; don't force or try to change anything, just notice.

- If your mind wanders, simply observe your thoughts then calmly redirect your attention back to your body.

- When you've finished, return your focus to your breath, then gently open your eyes and carry on with your day.

"Life is really simple,
but we insist on making
it complicated."

Confucius

"If you want to be happy, do not dwell in the past, do not worry about the future, focus on living fully in the present."

Roy T. Bennett

Create a mindful morning ritual

How do your mornings usually look? Unhurried and serene? Or do you throw on some clothes, gulp a coffee and fly out of the door? Mornings can be challenging, but they can also set the tone for the day. Here are some tips for a more mindful start …

- **Get ready the night before:** Simple actions like putting your clothes out, organising your work materials, making a packed lunch and knowing where your keys are can help set you up for the rest of the day.

- **Set your intentions:** Instead of automatically reaching for your phone when you wake up, write down your intentions for the day, or make a list of three things you're looking forward to.

- **Stretch:** Check in with your body with a few gentle roll-downs, shoulder shrugs and arm circles, if you are able.

- **Do a mini-meditation:** If you can't manage 30 minutes, then do three minutes instead.

- **Smell the coffee:** Don't just gulp it; use your senses to appreciate everything about it.

- **See the light:** Morning sunlight boosts the production of serotonin, inducing a calm state of mind. If you only do one thing in the morning, try to get outdoors – even if it's just for a few minutes.

"To experience peace does not mean that your life is always blissful. It means that you are capable of tapping into a blissful state of mind amidst the normal chaos of a hectic life."

Jill Bolte Taylor

"Almost everything will work again if you unplug it for a few minutes, including you."

Anne Lamott

Take a mindful approach to work

Mindfulness in the workplace might sound like a contradiction in terms: with long hours, tight deadlines and tricky colleagues, our jobs are often a source of stress and anxiety.

It's easy to blitz through work on autopilot, without being fully present. The following tips can help you take a more mindful approach to your working life.

Stay engaged. Whether you're sitting at a computer, cash-desk, or checkout, try to concentrate on what you are doing, rather than making plans for the weekend. This will improve your performance which in turn can increase your level of job satisfaction.

Remain neutral. When faced with a challenging situation or colleague, try not to react. Instead, calmly assess the situation without judgement. This can help you to stay calm and objective.

Avoid multi-tasking. Concentrate on one thing at a time, for example, by drawing up a time-line of what you need to do and when. This increases efficiency and reduces the risk of burnout.

Take breaks. Whether it's eating your lunch outdoors, or finding a quiet room to sit and meditate for a few minutes, taking time out to recharge makes you more productive in the long run.

> **Try this:** Use short mindfulness exercises to help calm your thoughts and increase your focus throughout your working day. You could do a breathing exercise before a meeting, a body scan at your desk, or a quick meditation during your lunch break. And no one need even know …

"There is virtue in work
and there is virtue in rest.
Use both and overlook neither."

Alan Cohen

"These mountains that you are carrying, you were only supposed to climb."

Najwa Zebian

Try a five-minute mantra meditation

Mindfulness and meditation are often used interchangeably. While mindfulness involves focusing your awareness on the present moment, meditation involves releasing your mind from distractions.

Some types of meditation are based around a mantra – a word, phrase or sound that you repeat silently to quieten your thoughts – such as 'om' or 'peace'. Try this simple mantra meditation.

- Sit comfortably, hands open, palms upwards. Either close your eyes or fix your gaze on a single object, like a candle or a picture.

- Take a few deep breaths – in through your nose and out through your mouth – to steady your breathing.

- 🌿 Silently repeat your mantra on each out breath, repeating it in your mind like a whisper.

- 🌿 Don't worry if other thoughts intrude; this is normal at first. Just let them go and return to your mantra.

- 🌿 As you enter a deeper level of awareness, you may not even need to say your mantra.

- 🌿 After five minutes, open your eyes and slowly return to your thoughts and surroundings.

You can find many more guided meditations online, or by downloading a mediation app.

"All men's miseries derive from not being able to sit in a quiet room alone."

Blaise Pascal

> "Life is a dance.
> Mindfulness is witnessing
> that dance."

Amit Ray

Enjoy a mindful eating exercise

Mindful eating is the practice of being fully present when we eat – of being aware of, and savouring, the food as we eat it. There are many benefits to mindful eating, not least that it can help improve our diet, regulate our appetite and aid weight loss.

If you often munch in front of the TV or at your desk, this exercise can encourage you to eat more mindfully.

- Take any food you enjoy.

- Bring your awareness to your food, as if seeing it for the first time. Take in all the details: colour, shape, texture, size, smell, weight.

- Notice your thoughts, emotions and sensations, such as hunger, thirst, or even guilt.

- Think about your food's journey – from seed or factory to supermarket and plate. Take a moment to acknowledge all the people involved in bringing you this food.

- Next, use your fingers to explore how it feels. Is it sticky, soft, hard, smooth or lumpy?

- Lift the food towards your nose. How does it smell? Does it remind you of anything?

- Place the food in your mouth. Explore it with your tongue, noticing its texture, flavour, temperature. Now chew, using your full awareness to focus on the taste. How does it make you feel? Notice any thoughts that enter your mind.

The next time you eat a normal meal, recall this exercise. Eating mindfully helps prevent overeating by making you more aware of portion size and when you are full.

"To eat is a necessity, but to eat intelligently is an art."

François de la Rochefoucauld

Try a loving-kindness meditation

Send good vibes to yourself and others with this loving-kindness meditation. It might seem strange at first, but this type of meditation is a scientifically proven way to boost compassion and wellbeing.

So, get comfy, close your eyes and, starting with yourself, repeat the following in your mind.

May I be happy.
May I be well.
May I be safe.
May I find peace.

Now, think about someone you care about, such as a friend or family member. Picture them, feel their presence, say their name and repeat the meditative words.

May you be happy.
May you be well.
May you be safe.
May you find peace.

Next, think of someone you don't know very well, perhaps a neighbour or an acquaintance, and do the same for them.

Finally, think of someone you don't get on well with and direct the meditation towards them. You may feel hurt or resentful. That's perfectly natural; just recognise your own feelings, and allow yourself to let them go, as an act of love and compassion for yourself.

When you're ready, open your eyes and return to your day. With practice, loving-kindness meditations will transform how you relate to others and yourself.

"Kindness can become its own motive. We are made kind by being kind."

Eric Hoffer

"What we all have in
common is an appreciation
of kindness and compassion;
all the religions have this.
Love.
We all lean towards love."

Richard Gere

Embrace nature

Imagine if there was a natural antidepressant, or a powerful tranquiliser that didn't have any adverse side effects. It sounds too good to be true, but the answer is all around us. A colossal amount of research shows that nature does wonders for our wellbeing. Here are just some of the perks.

- **Your stress levels will fall:** Being in nature has a calming effect that relieves feelings of anxiety and helps lower your blood pressure.

- **Your happiness levels will rise:** The mood-boosting properties of green spaces are known to alleviate symptoms of mild to moderate depression.

- **It provides a mental health buffer:** As well as helping to combat depression, spending time in nature reduces the chance of developing it in the first place.

- **You'll be more focused:** Fresh air helps you to unplug, increasing your attention span.

- **It's a natural way to get fit:** Being outdoors often involves physical activity, which is good for the rest of your health, too.

- **It contributes to a sense of purpose:** People who feel more connected with nature are more likely to describe their lives as worthwhile.

"Flowers always make
people better, happier,
and more hopeful;
they are sunshine, food,
and medicine for the soul."

Luther Burbank

"Some old-fashioned
things like fresh air
and sunshine
are hard to beat."

Laura Ingalls Wilder

Step outside

As you've just discovered, there is no greater antidote to the stresses of modern life than immersing yourself in the great outdoors. When the world feels manic and out of control, nature reminds us to slow down and take a breath; to stop doing and simply be.

The good news is that you can find nature wherever you are – whether that's a windswept hill in the middle of nowhere or a well-kept park in the middle of a city. So, make a date with nature now! Use the opportunity to be fully present in the natural world and experience an innate sense of wellbeing.

- **Tune in to your senses:** Accept nature's invitation to notice the rustle of leaves, the smell of the earth, the sound of birdsong, shards of sunlight streaming through clouds.

- **Notice your surroundings:** Take a moment to observe the things in front of your eyes: the symmetry of a leaf, a bee resting on a flower, a weed poking through concrete.

- **Ground yourself:** When the modern world feels fragmented and disjointed, remind yourself of the continuity of nature: the permanence of the sky, the phases of the moon, the rhythm of the seasons. You are part of nature, not separate from it.

"Look deep into nature,
and then you
will understand
everything better."

Albert Einstein

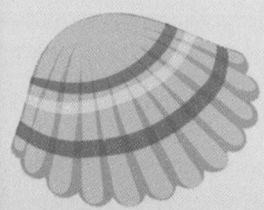

"If you truly love nature,
you will find beauty
everywhere."

Vincent van Gogh

Bring the outdoors in

When it comes to being mindful in nature, there's no substitute for actually getting outdoors. However, when that's not possible, bringing the outdoors in can be the next best thing.

Houseplants are a delightful way to enhance your wellbeing and your living environment at the same time. Plus, you'll be able to impress your friends with your botanical knowledge (it's a *Monstera*, not a Swiss cheese plant!) and show off your eye for interior design. What's more, many indoor plants help remove harmful toxins from the air.

Here are some gorgeous plants to boost your home and calm your mood.

- **Peace lily:** The name says it all. In addition to their elegant looks and calming presence, peace lilies also remove indoor pollution.

- **Lavender:** This plant is loved for its distinctive, soothing aroma. Keep some in the bedroom to aid relaxation.

- **English ivy:** This looks wonderful and is one of the best plants for reducing indoor mould levels.

- **Monstera:** A great choice for a statement piece; the large, shiny leaves help balance humidity levels.

- **Spider plants:** These air-purifying plants are a doddle to look after … and they reproduce like horticultural rabbits.

"If you look the right way,
you can see that the
whole world is a garden."

Frances Hodgson Burnett

Just walk

With the dizzying array of wellness trends on offer, it can be easy to overlook the simple power of just going for a walk. As well as being great exercise, walking is a wonderful way to practise mindfulness: you just need to tune in to yourself and your surroundings. Be present in the moment: make yourself aware of the way your body moves as you walk and focus on the beauty in the world around you.

Here are some more reasons to get your walking shoes on.

- **It's brilliant for your health:** Walking lowers the risk of numerous conditions, including heart disease, type 2 diabetes, depression and even dementia. It also promotes bone density, reducing the risk of fractures and osteoporosis.

- **It does wonders for your wellbeing:** Walking is a great stress-reliever and mood-enhancer, and is known to help alleviate depression and anxiety.

- **Injuries are rare:** Walking improves fitness without placing your body under undue stress. You're far less likely to pull or strain something by going for daily walks than by taking up running.

- **It blows away the cobwebs:** Moving at your own pace helps you to slow down and sort through your thoughts. Outside, we often see things in a different light.

- **It's free:** Well, unless you count the cost of shoes …

- **It's green:** No carbon footprints to see here!

"Walk towards the good in life and one day you will arrive."

Atticus

"All truly great thoughts are conceived while walking."

Friedrich Nietzsche

Take a moment to visualise

There are times when we all crave a few moments of peace. When running away to a spa isn't an option, use this visualisation exercise as a shortcut to serenity. Racing thoughts be gone …

- Find a quiet spot and sit or lie down comfortably, with your legs and arms uncrossed.

- Close your eyes and summon up a beautiful place in your mind – perhaps a soothing forest, a golden sun-drenched beach, or a meadow swathed in a rainbow of wild flowers.

- Sketch the details in your imagination – the whisper of the trees, the kiss of the waves brushing the sand, the colours of the flowers. You feel safe, calm and happy.

- Allow the tension in your head and face to dissolve.

- Place one hand on your chest and one on your belly; notice your breathing slowing down.

- Keep breathing deeply while focusing on your beautiful place, engaging all your senses to bring it to life.

- When you're ready, open your eyes and take two more breaths before returning to your day.

Use this exercise to return to your special place whenever you need a moment of escapism.

"Let your soul stand cool and composed before a million universes."

Walt Whitman

"Find a place inside where there's joy, and the joy will burn out the pain."

Joseph Campbell

Get lost in a story

Whether you're into historical fiction, romance, adventure or psychological thrillers, losing yourself in a good book provides a world of benefits. Research shows that reading increases empathy, improves memory, knowledge and concentration, and reduces stress. It can even lower the risk of Alzheimer's disease.

Reading for pleasure also helps us to block out the world around us, in a similar way to mindfulness and meditation. Here are some ways to feed your inner bookworm.

- **Join your local library:** Discover a world of books and more.

- **Join a book group:** You could even start your own if there isn't one locally.

- **Consider an audio book subscription:** Audio books are

great for walks, long journeys – and for when you can't find your glasses.

- **Follow book recommendations online and on social media:** Try platforms such as BookTok – a community of book fans on TikTok.

- **Visit a literary festival:** Literary festivals are great places to meet authors, listen to book talks and hang out with like-minded people.

- **Visit your local bookshop:** They will be grateful for your support and you never know what you might discover.

> **Try this:** Reading out loud can help you to slow down and focus on the sound and meaning of the words, which makes for an even more mindful experience.

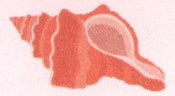

"A room without books
is like a body
without a soul."

Marcus Tullius Cicero

"Stories are the most important thing in the world. Without stories, we wouldn't be human beings at all."

Philip Pullman

Try a grounding technique

Grounding techniques bring us back to the present and help us reconnect with our body, reducing feelings of hypervigilance or anxiety.

Take a moment now to try this 5−4−3−2−1 method.

1. Notice five things you can see: Look around you and bring your awareness to five things you can see right now. Try to find things you wouldn't normally pay attention to, such as a reflection, a speck of dirt, a stray thread.

2. Notice four things you can touch: Focus on four things you can currently feel, such as the clothes against your skin, the chair you're sitting on, the air against your face.

3. Notice three things you can hear: Listen – what sounds are happening in the background? The hum of traffic, distant chatter, the wind outside?

4. Notice two things you can smell: Inhale – what can you smell? Notice pleasant or unpleasant smells, such as cooking odours, traffic fumes, your own perfume, the scent of cut grass.

5. Notice one thing you can taste: Focus on one thing you can taste in this moment. You could take a sip of water, chew gum, suck a sweet, or just open your mouth and taste the air.

"Be where you are, not where you think you should be."

Unknown

"Mindfulness is a pause
– the space between
stimulus and response:
that's where choice lies."

Tara Brach

Take up yoga

Yoga is one of the key practices of mindfulness, and there are many great reasons to include it in your lifestyle. It improves flexibility and balance, reduces stress and anxiety, and helps you to feel more peaceful and positive in the rest of your life, too. Recent research suggests what yogis have known for millennia: that yoga is hugely beneficial to our overall wellbeing.

Yoga originated in India around 5,000 years ago and is now widely practised all around the world. But there's more to yoga than just downward dogs and bamboo clothing. In Sanskrit, the word yoga means 'union', reflecting the way the practice helps bring the mind and body into harmony through poses, deep breathing and meditation.

As well as relieving physical and mental tension, yoga deepens your awareness, encouraging you to become more in tune with your body and its signals. By developing a regular yoga habit, you can transfer these benefits to your daily life, improving physical and mental wellbeing. And with more than 100 different styles, there's a form to suit everyone.

If you can't join a class, try following a guided workout video online.

"Yoga does not just change the way we see things, it transforms the person who sees."

B.K.S. Iyengar

"The best cure for the body is a quiet mind."

Napoleon Bonaparte

Have a mindful hug

There's nothing like a great big bear hug to make you feel all warm and fuzzy on the inside. Having a hug is also a lovely way to calm an agitated mind.

Research shows that hugging increases levels of oxytocin, also known as the 'love hormone'. This feel-good hormone is associated with positive emotions like trust, happiness and bonding.

As well as delivering a surge of happiness, oxytocin also helps counteract stress and anxiety. So, hugs don't just feel good, they're good for your health, too. The secret is not to let go too soon; research suggests that for maximum effect a hug should last at least 20 seconds. And, of course, both people sharing the hug will benefit.

Hugging isn't the only way to experience oxytocin. The hormone plays an important role in childbirth and breastfeeding. It's also involved with sexual attraction and desire, and it is released during orgasm.

> **Did you know?**
> Stroking a dog or a cat has also been shown to release oxytocin, as well as decreasing levels of the stress hormone cortisol. Research has even shown that watching fish in a tank or aquarium can boost our mood and lower our blood pressure.

"A problem shared is a problem halved. A joy shared is a joy doubled."

Unknown

"Happiness quite unshared can scarcely be called happiness; it has no taste."

Charlotte Bronte

Make mindfulness part of your daily life

We often associate mindfulness with structured techniques, such as yoga, meditation, visualisation and breathing exercises. However, mindfulness doesn't have to be a formal activity; you can be mindful while engaged in many ordinary tasks – and even household chores. The key is to remain fully present and aware. Try to be wholly engaged in whatever you are doing to prevent your thoughts from wandering. But if you notice your mind taking a detour, just bring it back to your task.

Incorporating mindfulness into your daily routine is a powerful way to improve your mental wellbeing. Here are some activities that naturally lend themselves to mindfulness.

- Going for a stroll
- Crafting
- Colouring or doodling
- Journaling
- Baking

- Listening to music
- Gentle gardening
- Sitting outside with your favourite drink
- Daydreaming
- Stroking a pet
- Watching the clouds
- Visiting an art gallery
- Taking a bath
- Having a lie down

> **Try this:** Introduce mindfulness to your daily chores, too: when washing the dishes, focus on the warm, flowing water; when hanging out the washing, notice the smell and texture of the fabrics. Be aware of your breathing and use your breath to keep you anchored in the moment and to help you keep calm and focused.

"The happiness of life is made up of minute fractions – the little, soon-forgotten charities of a kiss, a smile, a kind look ... and the countless other infinitesimals of pleasant thought and genial feeling."

Samuel Taylor Coleridge

"Rest is not idleness, and to lie sometimes on the grass under trees on a summer's day, listening to the murmur of the water, or watching the clouds float across the sky, is by no means a waste of time."

John Lubbock

Become a glimmer seeker

Searching for glimmers is another mindful way to notice the good that surrounds you. Glimmers are micro-moments of joy that help us to feel calm, safe and connected; they are the opposite to triggers, which can prompt the body to initiate the 'fight or flight' response.

Noticing glimmers increases our awareness of the present moment and encourages us to pay attention to all of our senses.

Try to find two or three glimmers a day and to notice the bodily sensations they evoke, such as the way your shoulders drop or the way the hairs on the back of your neck stand on end.

Glimmers can be very personal to an individual – and what works for one person may not work for another. Here are some things that can activate glimmers.

- Stroking a pet
- Cuddling a loved one
- A random act of kindness
- A shaft of light falling through a blind
- The feel of the breeze in your hair
- The warmth of the sun on your shoulders
- A song that gives you goosebumps
- The smell of a favourite perfume or essential oil
- Birdsong
- Blossom
- The sound of falling rain
- Bulbs pushing through the earth
- A beautiful sky

"HAPPINESS IS MAKING THE MOST OF WHAT YOU HAVE, AND RICHES IS MAKING THE MOST OF WHAT YOU'VE GOT."

Rosamunde Pilcher

"Simplicity is the ultimate sophistication."

Leonardo da Vinci

Let go of grudges

Developing a mindful mindset involves training ourselves to live in the present. Sometimes, in order to do this, we need to practise forgiveness. That's because when we hold grudges we remain anchored to the past. And when we harbour ill feelings, we remain hostage to our thoughts; we are imprisoned by hurt and anger. Mindfulness helps us to let these thoughts and feelings go.

Learning to forgive can be a long and difficult process. Yet in clinging to hurt and resentment we deprive ourselves of inner peace. However, in some cases forgiveness can feel like too much to ask; there are some actions which seem simply unforgiveable. If this is something you relate to; then do seek professional support, for example from a counsellor or therapist, rather than trying to move forward alone.

One way to think about letting go of a grudge is to see it as an act of self-compassion and a way of setting yourself free. Sometimes, forgiveness is more about doing something for yourself than it is for the other person. And remember, it doesn't have to be a reconciliation; forgiveness can simply be a way to draw a line under a situation so that you can move on.

> **Try this:** You may find it helpful to direct a loving-kindness meditation towards someone who has wounded or upset you. This may help you to put things behind you and start to find peace.

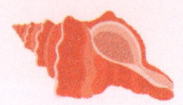

"If you are broken, you do not have to stay broken."

Selena Gomez

"Forgive others,
not because they deserve
forgiveness, but because
you deserve peace."

Jonathan Lockwood Huie

Tidy home, tidy mind

When we're surrounded by clutter, our minds can feel cluttered, too. So, having a sort out can help restore a sense of calm – both inside and out. What's more, the processes of decluttering can be a mindful activity in itself.

Here's a decluttering technique to try.

- Decide what you'd like to sort out, such as a bedroom, wardrobe or your shoe collection.

- Take everything out and put it in a pile on the floor.

- Place anything you definitely don't need or want on a 'rejection' pile.

- Return to your original pile. Pick up each item and ask

yourself whether you really love it, or whether it serves any purpose. If yes, place it on a 'keep' pile. If not, place it on the rejection pile. Create a separate 'don't know' pile, if necessary.

- Return the items from the keep pile to their original home – neatly!

- Divide the contents of the rejection pile into three groups: give away/sell; repair/recycle; throw away.

- Place the contents of the don't know pile into a box and store it out of sight. If you haven't touched it in six months, get rid of it.

"Clutter is nothing more than postponed decisions."

Barbara Hemphill

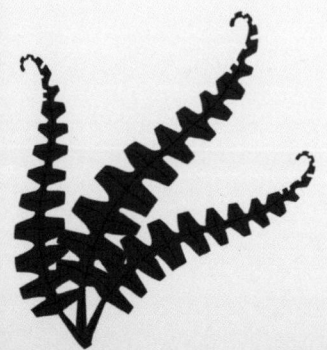

Put down your phone

We've all done it: scrolled through someone else's shiny social media feed – showcasing all their incredible holidays, amazing parties and blissful relationships – only to end up feeling like our own life is dull and empty in comparison. (And this is despite knowing that most people only post the extremely edited highlights of their life story.)

Mindless scrolling and doomscrolling (excessively scrolling through large quantities of negative news) have been linked to feelings of anxiety, depression and loneliness. But by adopting a more mindful approach, we can develop a heathier relationship with our phones.

1. Notice the negative effects that scrolling has on your life.

2. Streamline your social media. You don't have to come off completely (unless of course you want to) but decluttering your feed can help declutter your mind too. Remove people you don't want to engage with and prioritise real friends by exiting chat groups that zap your time and energy.

3. Consciously reduce your screen time. Try setting time limits, putting your phone on silent in the evenings and making an effort to swap scrolling for more mindful activities like baking, going for a walk, sketching, writing, or playing a game (not on your phone).

"No posting,
no liking,
just living."

Unknown

"I would say for my generation, specifically, social media has really been terrible. It does scare me when you see how exposed these young boys and young girls are ... I would be careful and allow yourself some time limits of when you should use it."

Selena Gomez

Try savouring

Savouring is the art of lingering in an uplifting moment – and it's a great tool to have in the mindfulness toolkit. Prolonging a positive experience roots us in the present and encourages us to notice how we are feeling; we can become absorbed in the details of the moment, which helps to draw us away from negative thoughts and distractions. We can savour moments in the past, present and future.

- **Savour the now:** Savouring can increase your appreciation of the world. It doesn't have to be anything extraordinary; you could savour the colours of an autumn walk, the appearance of a full moon or the smell and taste of your favourite ice cream.

- **Savour the past:** Think back to a treasured childhood experience, a favourite holiday or an amazing meal. Close your eyes and conjure up all the colour and emotions you experienced. See if you find yourself reliving those positive feelings.

- **Savour the future:** Think about something you are looking forward to. It could be catching up with friends, a birthday or just chilling on the sofa when you get home from work. Anticipating pleasant events can boost your mood in the present. And when the moment arrives, you will get to savour it all over again!

> "Forever – is composed of Nows."
>
> *Emily Dickinson*

"Maybe life is all about twirling under one of those midnight skies, cutting a swathe through the breeze and gently closing your eyes."

Sanober Khan

Flex your gratitude muscle

Gratitude is a great way to support mindfulness since it encourages us to become more aware of all the positive things around us.

Research shows that feeling thankful also boosts our serotonin levels, increasing feelings of wellbeing. Studies by the psychologist Dr Robert A. Emmons, the world's leading scientific expert on gratitude, have shown that people who regularly feel grateful, experience greater health and happiness than those who don't. Just taking 10 minutes a day to notice the good things in your life – and to recognise and acknowledge the source of these good things – can calm stress and boost your happy hormones.

Practising gratitude is easy when life is going well, but it's even more useful when you're having a hard time. Try following these steps.

- Think of a time you felt truly thankful.

- How did it make you feel?

- Now try to relive the moment, paying particular attention to the details.

- How do you feel now?

> **Try this:** Keep a gratitude journal to help make gratitude part of your mindset. Every night, write down three things – no matter how small – that you're thankful for. For example: someone in your life who supports you, your health, a pet, a meal you enjoyed or an act of kindness you received.

"If with a pure mind
a person speaks or acts,
happiness follows like
a shadow."

Buddha

"Knowing something is not as good as liking it. Liking something is not as good as rejoicing in it."

Confucius

Try a progressive muscle relaxation

This is a useful technique for alleviating both muscle tension and anxiety. It can be done either lying down or sitting upright. So, grab a comfy spot, take a few deep breaths, and try this relaxation.

- **Feet:** Bring your toes towards you. Hold, then release. Now point them. Hold, then let go. Continue to breathe slowly and evenly.

- **Legs and buttocks:** Squeeze your calves and quads as hard as you can, then release. Clench your buttocks, then let go.

- **Arms and hands:** One side at a time, ball your hand into a fist and bend it towards your forearm, feeling the tension. Now release. Flex the muscles in your arm, then let it fall limp.

- **Chest and stomach:** Take a deep breath, fill your lungs, tense your ribcage and upper back. Hold, then let go. Tighten your stomach muscles, pause, then release.

- **Neck and shoulders:** Raise your shoulders to your ears. Pause, then let go. Carefully tense your neck muscles and release.

- **Face:** Clench your jaw, purse your lips, wrinkle your forehead, raise your eyebrows, then let it all go.

Give yourself a moment to come round, notice how different you feel, then enjoy the rest of your day.

"Just when you feel you have no time to relax, know that this is the moment you most need to relax."

Matt Haig

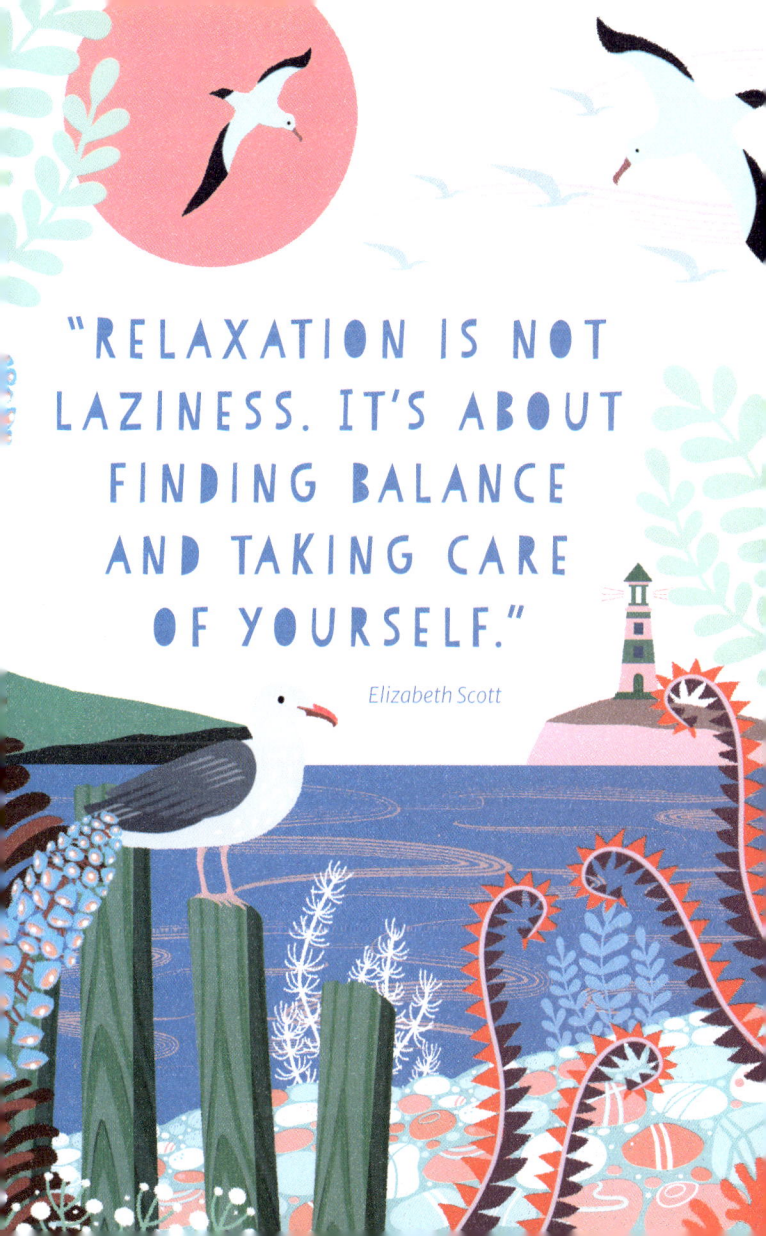

"RELAXATION IS NOT LAZINESS. IT'S ABOUT FINDING BALANCE AND TAKING CARE OF YOURSELF."

Elizabeth Scott

Reconnect with your childhood

If you've ever watched a young child at play, you'll know that children have a natural capacity for mindfulness. No matter what's happening around them, they can switch off from the outside world to become fully absorbed in whatever they're doing. This, combined with a natural sense of wonder, keeps them firmly rooted in the present – it's the holy grail of mindfulness. If only it was so easy once we reach adulthood.

Think back to your own childhood. Which activities did you enjoy? You might find that rediscovering old hobbies brings that childhood joy flooding back and helps you to be more mindful.

Here are some activities you might have done as a child. Why not give them another go?

- Doing a jigsaw
- Making a daisy chain
- Drawing
- Colouring
- Pebble-painting
- Story-writing
- Dancing
- Jewellery-making
- Lego
- Den-building
- Shell-collecting
- Model-making
- Stamp-collecting
- Playing with animals
- Swinging on a swing

"Growing old is mandatory;
growing up is optional."

Chili Davis

"There are no
seven wonders of the
world in the eyes
of a child. There are
seven million".

Walt Steightiff

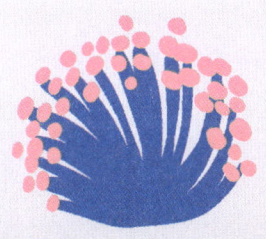

Try journaling

Even if you don't consider yourself to be much of a writer, journaling is an effective tool to support mindfulness. Keeping a journal helps you to observe your thoughts and feelings, and it can increase your sense of self-awareness.

Research also suggests that journaling can improve your wellbeing by reducing stress and boosting your mood. Here are some more good reasons to put pen to paper.

- Journaling promotes self-reflection, leading to personal growth and discovery.

- A journal is a useful way to process your thoughts and feelings.

- Keeping a journal before going to bed can help you to worry less at night, which will enable you to fall asleep faster.

- Recording situations and events in detail can help you to identify and understand your triggers.

- Seeing your fears and worries in black and white can encourage you to view them in a more objective way – they might even feel smaller on paper.

- A journal allows you to capture life's moments and provides something for you to look back on in the future.

There is no one rule for successful journaling; the form and process will be different for everyone, so just find a way that suits you.

Try free writing

Some people find free writing can be a very meditative activity as it allows you to go where your mind takes you. Don't think, just write whatever comes into your head – no one else needs to read it so embrace the freedom it offers!

> "All the noise in my brain.
> I clamp it to the page
> so it will be still."
>
> *Barbara Kingsolver*

"The very act of writing it down made her realize how easy it would be to forget, how important it would be from now on to put everything, everything, down on paper."

Donna Tartt

Take the plunge

Unless you've been living in the Sahara Desert for the past few years, you've probably heard about the cold water swimming craze. This (very) chilly activity has been gaining fans all around the globe.

Immersing yourself in open water takes mindfulness to another level, providing the ultimate sensory experience – a kind of mindfulness on steroids. In the water, you're not just in tune with the environment, but actually part of it; fully present and free from all worldly stresses as your brain focuses all its attention on the coldness of the water and its physical effect on your body.

If the very idea is enough to send you running for the nearest radiator, you might be interested to know that research suggests cold water swimming can help with a variety of conditions, including inflammation, high blood pressure, type 2 diabetes and depression. Wild swimmers often report feeling a 'post-swim high', and it's thought that cold water triggers a surge of dopamine, serotonin and endorphins.

If you don't live near any open water, a cold shower can provide some of the same benefits.

> If you have any medical conditions, seek advice first and always swim in open water with others.

"The sea, once it casts its spell, holds one in its net of wonder forever."

Jacques Yves Cousteau

"The ocean makes me feel really small and it makes me put my whole life into perspective."

Beyoncé

Try mindful swimming

If you don't fancy cold water swimming, then swimming at a more comfortable temperature can also be a deeply mindful activity.

Humans have a natural affinity with water. It soothes the stresses and strains of life, eases aches and pains, and instils us with a sense of calm and wellbeing. Have you ever looked out across a lake and felt your shoulders drop? Or been for a swim in your local pool and felt the rest of the world slide away? Here are some tips to help transform your swim into a relaxing, meditative experience.

- Focus on the sensation of floating, the freedom of weightlessness; concentrate on being fully present in the water.

- Notice the physical sensations: the rush of water past your ears, the temperature against your skin.

- Concentrate on your breath: allow the air to flow smoothly in and out of your lungs.

- Bring your awareness to the rhythm of your stroke, the smooth, repetitive motion of your limbs propelling you forwards. How does it feel?

- Slow down, relax, find a pace you can sustain.

- Allow your mind to empty, letting thoughts and distractions float away as you swim up and down.

"A river seems a magic thing.
A magic, moving, living part
of the very earth itself."

Laura Gilpin

Press pause

We live in a culture obsessed with productivity. Take the hashtag #5to9routine, for example. The craze, which sees people waking up at 5am to cram even more into their already exhausting routines, has amassed millions of views on TikTok.

In our goal-driven world, it can be easy to feel like we're wasting time when we're not moving at 100 kilometres per hour – or sharing our extreme wake-up regime on social media.

However, making time for stillness is an important part of developing a mindful mindset.

Pressing pause helps us to navigate the demands of the crazy world we live in – and it's in the small, unhurried moments that we find space for growth and clarity. So, take a few moments now, to find stillness.

- Recognise your feelings.
- Notice your thoughts.
- Become aware of how you are reacting.
- Breathe into yourself to create space.
- Inhale and say the word 'let' in your mind.
- Exhale and say the word 'go' in your mind.
- Repeat these breaths five more times.

Do this whenever you feel like you are being pulled in multiple directions at once.

"Laziness is nothing more than the habit of resting before you get tired."

Jules Renard

"You are allowed to rest."

Unknown

Take a mindful rest

We often equate rest with sleeping, but there are seven types of rest that we all need for physical and mental wellbeing. The important thing is to realise that rest is not an indulgence; it's something that we, as humans, actually need – so make rest intentional and embrace it as a way to revive yourself.

- **Physical rest:** As well as sleeping or having a power nap, physical rest could also be something that soothes your body, such as getting a massage.

- **Mental rest:** This gives your brain a break from constant stimulation. Why not turn off your phone or try a short meditation?

- **Creative rest:** This type of rest could involve engaging in a mindful hobby or spending time in nature. It's especially important if you have a demanding, creative job.

- **Emotional rest:** This is about setting boundaries, especially in relation to emotionally draining events and people.

- **Social rest:** Human connections are vital, but time alone is important, too – especially for introverts.

- **Sensory rest:** A constant barrage of noise, screens and lights can lead to sensory overload, so take a sensory rest by having a digital detox.

- **Spiritual rest:** Resting spiritually is about creating space to connect to something larger than yourself. If you're not religious, you could achieve spiritual rest by experiencing awe in the natural world.

"Nature does not hurry,

yet everything

is accomplished."

Lao Tzu

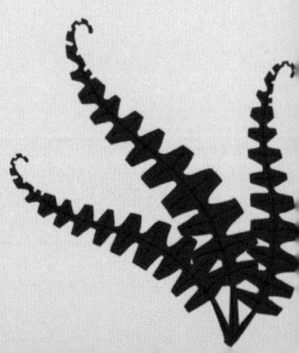

"It takes courage
to say yes to rest
and play in a culture
where exhaustion
is seen as a
status symbol."

Brené Brown

Let go of self-judgement

Mindfulness encourages us to bring our awareness to our own thoughts without judgement. Yet how many times a day do you criticise yourself? Or tell yourself you should or shouldn't have done something?

It's normal to judge ourselves. But when we pay attention to the negative voice inside our heads, it's easy to end up believing those thoughts, which can lead to shame and unhappiness.

Practising mindfulness helps us to acknowledge that thoughts are simply thoughts, not facts. This gives us the power to let them go, reducing their hold over us.

Try this exercise to free yourself from self-judgement.

- When your inner critic appears, recognise the thoughts in your head.

- Notice what is happening, becoming aware of both your body and emotions.

- Investigate everything as if you were an outside observer.

- Breathe deeply and say to yourself: "That's a judgement. I can let it go."

Learning to do this takes time and practice. Remind yourself that mindfulness is not a goal, but an ongoing process. By nurturing a mindful approach to life, you will develop a greater compassion for both yourself and others.

"You are the sky.
Everything else – it's
just the weather."

Pema Chödrön

"Nothing is worth more than this day. You cannot relive yesterday. Tomorrow is still beyond your reach."

Johann Wolfgang von Goethe

Two breathing exercises to try

Once you've got the hang of belly breathing (covered earlier in this book), you might like to try these slightly more advanced techniques to help you feel calm and focused. Both of these exercises work by calming the nervous system which helps to reduce anxiety levels.

Box breathing
For this technique, imagine you are following the four sides of a square with your breathing pattern. So:

- Inhale for a count of four seconds.

- Hold your breath for a count of four.

- Exhale for a count of four.

- Hold your breath for a count of four.

- Repeat a few more times.

4–7–8 breathing

For this exercise, don't worry about the speed at which you count, just try to keep an even pace to maintain the 4:7:8 ratio. This is a good technique to try if you have trouble falling asleep at night.

- Place the tip of your tongue just behind your upper front teeth.

- Close your mouth and inhale through your nose for a count of four.

- Hold your breath for a count of seven.

- Exhale through your mouth, making a whooshing sound for a count of eight.

- Repeat the cycle three more times.

> "For breath is life,
> and if you breathe well
> you will live long on earth."

Sanskrit proverb

"Breathing in, I calm body and mind. Breathing out, I smile. Dwelling in the present moment I know this is the only moment."

Thích Nhất Hạnh

Try a barefoot mindfulness exercise

Do you remember running around, barefoot, as a child? Remember that wonderful sense of freedom and joy without the confinement of leather and laces?

Going barefoot isn't just for children. It's a wonderful way to experience your surroundings and practise mindfulness. Here's an exercise to help you do just that. It's best to do it on grass, earth or sand, but you could also try it indoors.

- Take off your shoes and socks, and plant your feet firmly on the ground.

- Take a minute to breathe, noticing how still and permanent the ground feels beneath your feet. Allow this stillness to seep into your mind.

- Begin walking. Use every part of your foot to make contact with the ground – your heel, arch, the ball of your foot, your toes. Purposefully roll through each step, focusing your awareness on the sensations you experience.

- To allow your feet and ankles to adapt, start with around 10 minutes and build up gradually.

> If going for a walk isn't an option, try sitting in a chair with your bare feet on the floor. Simply bring your attention to the solid ground beneath you to help to calm your mind.

"One of the great things about children is that they have no other concern than to be simply interested in things. It is considered by some the height of mindfulness to approach the world afresh like a child."

John Dickerson

"Once we believe in ourselves,

we can risk curiosity,

wonder, spontaneous delight,

or any experience that

reveals the human spirit."

E.E Cummings

Foods to reduce anxiety

Changing your diet won't solve all your problems. It won't pay your bills or fix your relationship; however, eating mindfully — by simply paying more attention to the foods you consume, engaging your senses and recognising hunger and fullness — will improve your mood, your energy levels and your overall wellbeing, giving you a greater capacity to deal with stress. Here are some foods to boost your inner calm.

- **Avocados and bananas:** These are rich in B vitamins that support the brain and nervous system and help with the production of feel-good hormones like serotonin. Other sources include nuts, seeds, asparagus and leafy greens.

- **Oatmeal:** Stress can tempt us to reach for the biscuit jar, causing a spike in blood sugar levels that is quickly followed by a crash. Better options include complex carbs like oatmeal and wholegrains, which give a slow release of energy.

- **Salmon:** Oily fish is high in omega-3 fatty acids, which are needed for brain function and mental health.

- **Brazil nuts:** These are a very rich source of selenium, which is thought to have mood-boosting properties. However, they should only be eaten in small quantities to avoid overdosing on the mineral.

- **Eggs:** As well as being a good source of protein, eggs provide vitamin D – a lack of which is linked to depression and anxiety. They also contain tryptophan, which helps with the production of serotonin.

"Take care of your body. It's the only place you have to live."

Jim Rohn

"HE WHO HAS HEALTH HAS HOPE, AND HE WHO HAS HOPE HAS EVERYTHING."

Arabian proverb

Mind your gut

The human gut is sometimes referred to as the 'second brain'. That's because your digestive system and your brain are physically connected by the vagus nerve and are in constant communication with each other. This explains why you get butterflies in your stomach when you're nervous.

Your gut is also home to your microbiome — an ecosystem of trillions of bacteria, yeasts and other microorganisms that are vital for good health. Recent evidence suggests that a healthy microbiome can also support your mental health, improving mood and reducing anxiety.

The key to looking after your microbiome is to eat a wide range of gut-friendly foods, including prebiotics and probiotics.

Prebiotics

These are the non-digestible nutrients in food that feed the good bacteria in your gut. They come from a variety of fibre-rich foods like onions, garlic, lentils, bananas and flaxseed.

Probiotics

These are beneficial live microorganisms that occur in fermented, or cultured, foods such as yogurt, kimchi, sauerkraut and kombucha.

> **Try this:** Eat 30 different types of plants a week to help improve your gut microbiome. As well as fruits and vegetables, this can include herbs, spices, beans, pulses, nuts and wholegrains – and even good-quality, dark chocolate!

"When diet is wrong,
medicine is of no use.
When diet is correct,
medicine is of no need."

Ayurvedic proverb

"You are what you eat,
so don't be fast, cheap,
easy or fake."

Unknown

Try probiotics

Probiotics have been the subject of much recent excitement as a result of their potential to support both gut health and mental health. However, fermented foods have been eaten by humans for centuries. Here are some to give your taste buds – and your digestive system – a boost.

- **Kombucha:** This is a sweetened, fermented, slightly effervescent black tea, originally from China. It is rich in gut-loving bacteria and yeast species.

- **Miso:** Miso is a delicious, gut-friendly paste made from fermented soybeans. It is guaranteed to pack a flavourful punch.

- **Yogurt:** Give the sugary yogurts a miss and look for those containing live cultures – or try making your own.

- **Apple cider vinegar (ACV):** ACV is made by crushing apples, then adding yeast to ferment the natural sugars. Unfiltered ACV has a cloudy appearance and is thought to be the most beneficial because it contains the 'mother'.

- **Sauerkraut:** German for 'sour cabbage', sauerkraut is made with finely sliced raw cabbage that's layered with salt and left to ferment. The fermentation process causes the natural sugars in the cabbage to create probiotic bacteria.

- **Kefir:** Kefir is a fermented milk drink, similar to yogurt. While it can be expensive to buy, it's fairly simple to make at home.

"Choose only one master
– Nature."

Rembrandt

"The doctor of the future will no longer treat the human frame with drugs, but rather will cure and prevent disease with nutrition."

Thomas Edison

Seven ways to feel instantly Zen

For when you just need a quick dose of calm, look no further than these blissfully soothing options ...

1. Listen to some ASMR (autonomous sensory meridian response) sounds: These are the sounds that trigger 'brain tingles', calming the nervous system and invoking a deep sense of relaxation.

2. Invest in a weighted blanket: The even distribution of weight exerts a gentle pressure on the body, helping to reduce levels of the stress hormone cortisol. And it feels like a gentle hug!

3. Try aromatherapy: Our scent pathway is directly linked to the brain. Research shows that essential oils help stimulate the parasympathetic nervous system, activating our relaxation response.

4. Massage your hands: Treat yourself to a gorgeous hand cream and soothe dry skin and a busy mind at the same time.

5. Light a scented candle: This will help to promote feelings of peace and tranquillity. Just don't leave it unattended …

6. Take a lavender bath: It's not just an old wives' tale – studies show that lavender can reduce stress.

7. Have a reflexology session: Any form of massage is wonderful, but a foot massage can be particularly relaxing as it stimulates the vagus nerve.

"Be happy in the moment, that's enough. Each moment is all we need, not more."

Mother Teresa

"Mindfulness gives you time. Time gives you choices. Choices, skillfully made, lead to freedom."

Bhante Henepola Gunaratana

Five steps towards a more mindful life

Mindfulness doesn't happen on its own. It takes positive action to nurture a mindful mindset and to calm racing thoughts. Aim to follow these steps as a way to live mindfully, with greater purpose and, ultimately, greater happiness.

1. Make time for reflection: Be aware of the things pulling you in multiple directions. What one thing can you change?

2. Make time for yourself: However busy you are, it's vital to schedule time out. Block off 10 calming minutes a day – whether that's a mini-meditation before work, a breathing exercise before bed, or a blast of fresh air before picking up the kids.

3. Make time for others: Strong relationships are fundamental to our overall wellbeing; spending time with others supports a healthy mind.

4. Be an opportunist: The beauty of mindfulness is that you can bring it to so many situations – waiting at traffic lights, eating a meal, doing the laundry, walking to work or school. Bring your awareness to daily tasks and notice how your mindset changes.

5. Check in with yourself: We often ask other people the question, "How are you?" However, it's a question we seldom ask ourselves. So, make a point of checking in with yourself, too.

"A lot of the time I call my mum and talk for a really long time, just to remind myself of all the things that are great and that matter."

Taylor Swift

"Adopt the pace of nature:

her secret is patience."

Ralph Waldo Emerson

And finally ...

Hopefully, this book has inspired you to embrace mindfulness in everything you do. Nurturing a mindful mindset will equip you to navigate modern life – and all its craziness – with peace and clarity. It will open your eyes, your thoughts, your senses and your awareness to the present moment.

Being fully present and focused in the moment will not only give you the resources to deal with stressful events, it will allow you to cherish the joy of living, without being held hostage to the past or caught up in the future.

We can't always escape the pressures and demands of the world we live in, but we can avoid being overwhelmed by them. It takes time and practice to make mindfulness not just something you do, but a part of who you are;

the benefits of doing so will enrich every area of your life. And there is no time like the present! So, use the techniques and practices covered in this book to continue your own mindfulness journey and regain peace and balance in your life.

"Cultivate peace of mind. When the mind is compassionate, it is calm and we're able to use our sense of reason practically, realistically, and with determination."

Dalai Lama